Published by Netivyah International
www.netivyahinternational.org
POB 1387
Mount Juliet, TN 37121

Introduction to the Weekly Reading Cycle

The History of the Parasha Cycle

The parasha cycle (weekly Torah reading cycle) developed in Jewish communities as a way to ensure that the entire Torah — the Five Books of Moses — would be read publicly in the synagogue every year. By dividing the Torah into 54 parashot (portions), the Jewish people could complete the Torah annually, beginning after the fall festival of Simchat Torah and concluding the following year.

This tradition has roots in the Second Temple period and was solidified in Babylonian Jewish communities around the 6th–7th centuries CE. Public reading of the Torah was already commanded in the days of Ezra and Nehemiah (Nehemiah 8:1–8), and the cycle ensured that Torah would remain central to Jewish worship, identity, and education across the diaspora.

Why Some Weeks Are Double Portions

Because the Hebrew calendar follows a lunar cycle, the number of Shabbats in a year can vary. Some years have 54 Sabbaths, allowing each parasha to be read separately. Other years have fewer Sabbaths (for example, when festivals like Passover or Sukkot fall on Shabbat and replace the regular Torah reading). To ensure the Torah is still completed in one year, certain readings are "doubled" together into one week. For example, Tazria and Metzora are often read together, as are Behar and Bechukotai. This keeps the cycle consistent while adjusting for the calendar's variations.

The Haftara Readings

Alongside each Torah portion, a passage from the Prophets (Nevi'im) — called the Haftara — is traditionally read. This practice dates back to the time when foreign rulers occasionally restricted public Torah readings. To preserve weekly gatherings around Scripture, prophetic passages with thematic ties to the Torah portion were chosen. Over time, the pairing of Torah and Haftara became a lasting tradition, reinforcing the unity of the Tanakh (Hebrew Bible).

<u>**The Development of New Testament Readings in the Messianic Jewish World**</u>

In the Messianic Jewish movement, beginning especially in the 20th century, many congregations sought to reconnect with the rhythms of traditional synagogue life. They reintroduced the weekly Torah and Haftara cycle, but added a third reading from the New Testament (Brit Hadashah).

This innovation reflects the conviction that the New Testament writings are deeply rooted in the Torah and Prophets. By pairing Apostolic writings with the parasha, Messianic believers highlight continuity rather than division between the covenants.

Over the past fifty years, reading cycles that connect Torah, Haftara, and Brit Hadashah have become widely used in Messianic congregations worldwide.

Returning to the Rhythm of the Word

The Rhythm of Scripture in the First Century

The synagogue of the first century was the beating heart of Jewish life. Beyond being a place of prayer, it was primarily a house of study and Scripture. Each Shabbat, the Torah was read aloud in Hebrew, then often explained or translated into the common language of the people — whether Aramaic or Greek. Following the Torah reading, a selection from the Prophets (the Haftara) was proclaimed, chosen because of its thematic connection.

The Gospels record Yeshua participating in this rhythm. In Luke 4:16–21, Yeshua enters the synagogue in Nazareth "as was His custom" and reads from the scroll of Isaiah. He did not invent a new practice of worship — He stepped into a well-established rhythm. The apostles did the same. Acts 13:14–15 describes Paul and Barnabas being invited to speak after the Torah and Prophets were read in the synagogue at Pisidian Antioch. The synagogue lectionary was the stage upon which the gospel was preached.

By contrast, many modern churches focus on a topical approach or highlight a single passage each week. While this can be meaningful, it often lacks the discipline of reading the whole counsel of God. Important sections of Scripture may be overlooked, and the sense of God's unfolding story can be fragmented. Returning to the synagogue model would ensure systematic exposure to the Word and would connect believers with the way Scripture was originally proclaimed in Yeshua's day.

Returning to the Rhythm of the Word

Why the Church Needs the Cycle Today

Hearing the Whole Story

A structured cycle prevents the neglect of less familiar texts. For example, Leviticus is rarely preached in churches, yet it is foundational for understanding holiness, atonement, and priesthood — all essential to appreciating Messiah's work. The parasha cycle forces the reader into conversations with every part of Scripture.

Forming Discipleship Rhythms

Part of Discipleship is living in rhythm with God's Word. The cycle creates habits — weekly readings at home, in congregations, and in small groups. Families grow together around the same texts, and communities walk in step with Israel worldwide, reading the same Torah portion. This builds unity and identity across cultures and denominations.

Recovering Continuity with Israel

Much of church history has been marked by separation from Jewish roots. The cycle bridges this gap. It affirms that the Scriptures of Israel remain central to the identity of Messiah's people. Reading Torah weekly alongside the New Testament declares that the "Old Testament" is not outdated but the living foundation upon which the New Testament stands.

Returning to the Rhythm of the Word

How It Enriches Faith in Yeshua

The cycle doesn't merely provide order – it highlights Messiah Himself.

Torah and Yeshua as the Living Word

Reading Torah reveals the holiness of God and the covenant framework. Yeshua, as the Word made flesh (John 1:14), fulfills and embodies this revelation. The cycle constantly places Him back into His own context.

Haftara and the Prophetic Voice

The prophets called Israel back to covenant faithfulness and pointed forward to redemption. When their words are read alongside the Torah and Brit Hadashah, Yeshua shines as the fulfillment of prophecy. Luke 24:27 tells us that Yeshua "beginning with Moses and all the Prophets, explained to them what was said in all the Scriptures concerning Himself."

Brit Hadashah and Apostolic Witness

The New Testament writings echo Torah and Prophets. For example, Hebrews cannot be grasped without Leviticus; Revelation cannot be understood without Exodus and the prophets. The cycle lets believers see the unity of the Testaments and understand Yeshua as the thread that ties them together.

Returning to the Rhythm of the Word

Returning to the Roots of First-Century Faith

The First Believers Walked in This Rhythm

The earliest communities of Yeshua-followers — both Jewish and Gentile — gathered in synagogues. Acts 15 shows Gentile believers learning Torah in the synagogue each Shabbat. For centuries, the rhythm of weekly readings shaped how believers understood Messiah.

A Pathway Back to Unity

The church's detachment from Jewish practice contributed to misunderstandings and even hostility toward Israel. Restoring the reading cycle can be part of healing this division. It brings Gentile believers back into step with Israel, while maintaining faith in Yeshua as Messiah.

Grafted-In Discipleship

Paul describes Gentiles as wild branches grafted into Israel's olive tree (Romans 11). What better way to live this truth than to read Scripture in the same rhythm as Israel? This practice embodies the unity of Jew and Gentile in Messiah — one people, nourished by the same root.

Returning to the Rhythm of the Word

A Call to Return

Reintroducing the synagogue cycle will not make the church "Jewish". For its own sake, recovering the discipleship practices of Yeshua and the apostles, will anchor communities in the fullness of Scripture, and draw near to Messiah through His Word.

By embracing this rhythm:

- The church hears the whole Word of God, not just fragments.

- Believers discover Yeshua throughout the Torah and Prophets, enriching faith.

- Communities reconnect with the roots of first-century faith, finding common ground with Israel and with the earliest disciples.

Elizabeth Shulam

October 2025

Key Words & Definitions

- **Parasha** (פָּרָשָׁה) – A weekly portion of the Torah (the first five books of the Bible) read in synagogue. There are 54 portions, ensuring the Torah is read annually.
- **Haftara** (הַפְטָרָה) – A passage from the Prophets read after the weekly Torah portion, chosen for thematic connection.
- **Torah** (תּוֹרָה) – The first five books of the Bible (Genesis–Deuteronomy), also called the "Law of Moses." Literally means "instruction" or "teaching."
- **Brit Hadashah** (בְּרִית חֲדָשָׁה) – Hebrew for "New Covenant." Refers to the New Testament writings.
- **Synagogue** (συναγωγή / Beit Knesset) – Jewish house of prayer, study, and gathering. In the first century, it was where Torah and Prophets were read and explained weekly.
- **Shabbat** (שַׁבָּת) – The Sabbath, the seventh day (Friday evening to Saturday evening), set apart for rest and worship according to the commandments.
- **Double Portion** – When two parashot are read together on one Shabbat to keep the yearly Torah cycle aligned with the Hebrew calendar.
- **Lectionary** – A structured schedule of Scripture readings for worship. The Jewish lectionary is the weekly parasha/haftara cycle; many Christian traditions also use lectionaries.
- **Messianic Judaism** – A movement of Jewish and Gentile believers who confess Yeshua (Jesus) as the Messiah while honoring the Jewish roots of faith and often practicing elements of Jewish tradition.
- **Yeshua** (יֵשׁוּעַ) – The Hebrew name of Jesus, meaning "salvation."
- **Tanakh** (תַּנַ״ךְ) – The Hebrew Bible, an acronym for Torah (Law), Nevi'im (Prophets), and Ketuvim (Writings). Christians call this the Old Testament.

Table of Contents

Genesis / Bereshit

Exodus / Shemot

Leviticus / Vayikra

Numbers / Bamidbar

Deuteronomy / Devarim

PARASHA

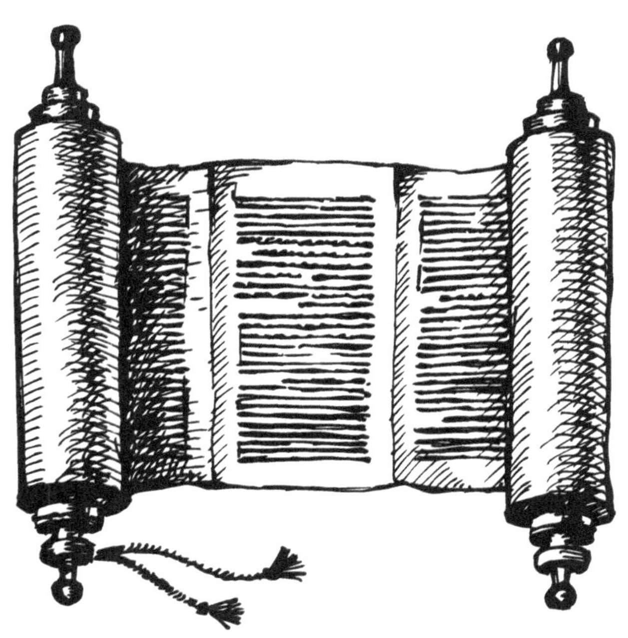

✦ BERESHIT ✦

GENESIS

Bereshit (Genesis) – "In the Beginning"

Introduction

Genesis tells the story of creation, humanity's fall, and the beginnings of God's covenant with Abraham, Isaac, Jacob, and Joseph. It lays the foundation for faith: God as Creator, humanity's need for redemption, and covenant promises that find fulfillment in Messiah Yeshua.

Historical Background

Traditionally, Genesis is attributed to Moses, written during Israel's wilderness journey. Ancient Jewish tradition holds that God revealed the primeval history (Genesis 1–11) directly, while the patriarchal narratives were preserved through oral tradition.

Modern Scholarship

Modern scholars often discuss Genesis in terms of source traditions. The Documentary Hypothesis (J, E, P, D)suggests Genesis was compiled from multiple strands:

J (Yahwist) emphasizes vivid narratives and anthropomorphic depictions of God.

E (Elohist) uses "Elohim" and stresses prophetic themes.

P (Priestly) highlights genealogies, creation order, and covenants.

While debated, these theories reflect that Genesis contains multiple literary styles, possibly edited during the Babylonian exile to reinforce covenant identity. For Believers, such scholarship underscores God's ability to weave diverse voices into one unified testimony of His covenant.

BERESHIT   פָּרָשַׁת בְּרֵאשִׁית

TORAH: GENESIS 1:1–6:8
HAFTARA: ISAIAH 42:5–43:10
NEW TESTAMENT: JOHN 1:1–18

The Torah begins with the creation account. God speaks the world into being, creating light, the heavens, the earth, and all living creatures. Humanity, made in God's image, is given responsibility to steward creation. Adam and Eve fall into sin, leading to exile from Eden. Cain kills his brother Abel, violence and corruption spread, and God resolves to judge the earth but identifies Noah as righteous in his generation.

Isaiah proclaims that the same Creator who formed the heavens also called Israel to be a light to the nations. God reassures His people of His covenant faithfulness and challenges them to turn away from idols and trust in Him.

John opens his gospel with echoes of Genesis: 'In the beginning was the Word.' He identifies Yeshua as the eternal Word through whom all creation came to be, the Light shining in darkness, and the One who reveals the Father to humanity.

CONNECTIONS

- God as Creator is the first theme that unites this week's Torah, Haftara, and John 1.

- The theme of light: physical light in creation, Israel a light to the nations, and spiritual light in Messiah.

- Humanity's fall and Messiah's role in restoration.

REFLECTION QUESTIONS

1. What does it mean to be created in the image of God in my daily life?

2. Where do I see the struggle between light and darkness today?

3. How does John 1 deepen my understanding of Genesis 1?

4. What can I learn from Noah's example of righteousness in a corrupt world?

NOACH

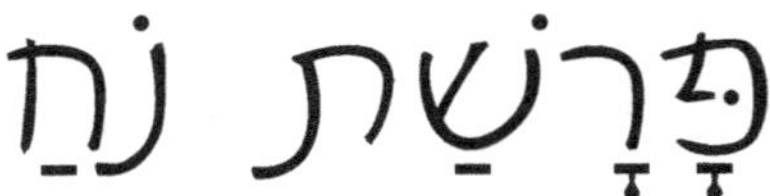

TORAH: GENESIS 6:9–11:32
HAFTARA: ISAIAH 54:1–55:5
NEW TESTAMENT: MATTHEW 24:36–44

Noah is chosen by God to survive the flood that
destroys a corrupt world. He builds the ark, gathers
his family and animals, and survives as the waters cover the
earth. After the flood, God makes a covenant with Noah, marked by the rainbow. The narrative
continues with the tower of Babel, humanity's prideful attempt to reach heaven, resulting in
God scattering them and confusing their languages.

Isaiah declares God's enduring covenant of peace. Though Israel has suffered, God
promises compassion and restoration, likening His covenant to the days of Noah when He
swore never again to flood the earth.

Yeshua compares the days of Noah to the coming of the Son of Man. Just as
people ignored God's warnings then, so too many will be unprepared for His return.
Believers are called to watchfulness and readiness.

CONNECTIONS

- God's covenant with Noah echoes Isaiah's promise of restoration.

- The flood and the scattering at Babel highlight God's justice and sovereignty.

- Messiah warns of vigilance, connecting Noah's story with end-times readiness.

REFLECTION QUESTIONS

1. What does the rainbow remind me about God's promises today?

2. How does the scattering at Babel relate to unity and diversity in God's plan?

3. What does Yeshua's warning about Noah's days mean for how I live?

4. Am I living with watchfulness and readiness for Messiah's return?

LECH LECHA 

TORAH: GENESIS 12:1–17:27

HAFTARA: ISAIAH 40:27–41:16

NEW TESTAMENT: ROMANS 4:1–25

God calls Abram to leave his homeland and promises to bless him, make him a great nation, and bless all families of the earth through him. Abram journeys to Canaan, builds altars, and trusts God's promises despite challenges. God makes a covenant with Abram, later c hanging his name to Abraham, and commands circumcision as a sign of the covenant.

Isaiah encourages Israel that God has chosen them, not abandoned them. Just as Abraham was called out, Israel is reminded that the Lord strengthens and upholds His people against fear and opposition. New Testament: Paul highlights Abraham as the model of faith, justified by trusting God's promises before circumcision or works of law.

Believers in Yeshua are heirs of the same promise through faith.

<u>CONNECTIONS</u>

- God's call of Abraham connects to Israel's identity in Isaiah.

- Faith as the foundation of righteousness: Abraham in Torah and Paul's teaching in Romans.

- The covenant sign of circumcision points to covenant relationship fulfilled in Messiah.

REFLECTION QUESTIONS

1. What does it mean for me to step out in faith like Abraham?

2. How do I see God's promises unfolding in my life despite obstacles?

3. What role does faith (not just works) play in my walk with God?

4. How can I be a blessing to others as Abraham was called to be?

TORAH: GENESIS 18:1–22:24
HAFTARA: 2 KINGS 4:1–37
NEW TESTAMENT: LUKE 17:28–37

Abraham receives three visitors who announce the birth of Isaac. God reveals
His plan to destroy Sodom and Gomorrah, and Abraham intercedes for the righteous.
Isaac is born, Hagar and Ishmael are sent away, and Abraham faces the ultimate test when God
commands him to sacrifice Isaac, which he obeys in faith until stopped by an angel.

Elisha miraculously provides for a widow and later raises the Shunammite
woman's son, echoing themes of promised children and God's power to give life.

Yeshua recalls the judgment of Sodom and warns of the suddenness of the
Son of Man's coming, calling for readiness and not looking back.

CONNECTIONS

- Promises of miraculous children: Isaac and the Shunammite's son.

- God's judgment on wickedness: Sodom and Yeshua's teaching.

- Faith and obedience: Abraham's test foreshadowing ultimate sacrifice in

  Messiah.

REFLECTION QUESTIONS

1. What can I learn from Abraham's intercession for others?

2. How do I respond when God asks me for costly obedience?

3. How does the Haftara remind me of God's power over life and death?

4. What does Yeshua's warning about Sodom mean for how I live today?

CHAYEI SARAH   פָּרָשַׁת חַיֵּי שָׂרָה

TORAH: GENESIS 23:1–25:18
HAFTARA: 1 KINGS 1:1–31
NEW TESTAMENT: MATTHEW 8:18–22

Sarah dies and Abraham purchases the cave of Machpelah as a burial site, affirming his faith in God's promise of the land. Abraham's servant is sent to find a wife for Isaac and, through prayer and divine guidance, meets Rebekah who willingly goes with him.
Abraham remarries, fathers more children, and dies, buried
alongside Sarah. Ishmael's genealogy is recorded.

David is old and near death, and his son Adonijah attempts to claim the throne.
Nathan and Bathsheba intervene, reminding David of God's promise, leading to Solomon being declared king.

Yeshua challenges followers to count the cost of discipleship, saying that
following Him requires leaving behind other priorities, echoing Rebekah's readiness to leave her family and follow God's plan.

<u>CONNECTIONS</u>

- Abraham's purchase of the burial site anchors faith in God's land promise.

- Rebekah's willing response mirrors discipleship themes in the NT.

- Leadership transition: Abraham to Isaac, David to Solomon, pointing to

  Messiah's eternal kingship.

REFLECTION QUESTIONS

1. How do Abraham's actions model faith in God's promises?

2. What does Rebekah's immediate obedience teach me about trusting God's call?

3. How do I respond when God asks me to leave comfort zones behind?

4. What does Solomon's appointment teach me about God's faithfulness to His promises?

TOLDOT

פָּרָשַׁת תּוֹלְדֹת

TORAH: GENESIS 25:19–28:9
HAFTARA: MALACHI 1:1–2:7
NEW TESTAMENT: ROMANS 9:6–16

Isaac and Rebekah pray for children, and God grants them twins, Esau and
Jacob. The struggle between them begins even in the womb. Esau sells his birthright to Jacob
for stew, and later Rebekah helps Jacob receive Isaac's blessing intended for Esau. Jacob
flees to avoid Esau's anger.

Malachi contrasts God's love for Jacob with His rejection of Esau's descendants,
affirming God's covenantal choice of Israel. The priests are reminded of their responsibility
to honor God's covenant.

New Testament: Paul explains that God's purposes are carried out through His sovereign
choice, highlighting Jacob and Esau as examples. Salvation is not based on human effort but
on God's mercy and calling.

CONNECTIONS

- Jacob and Esau show the theme of divine election and covenant.

- Malachi affirms God's covenant love for Jacob's line.

- Paul interprets Jacob and Esau as a picture of God's sovereign grace.

REFLECTION QUESTIONS

1. What does Jacob's story teach me about God's sovereignty in human lives?

2. How do I respond to God's mercy rather than relying on my own strength?

3. What responsibility do I carry as one chosen by God?

4. How does this passage shape my understanding of grace?

VAYETZEI 

TORAH: GENESIS 28:10–32:3
HAFTARA: HOSEA 12:13–14:10
NEW TESTAMENT: JOHN 1:43–51

Jacob dreams of a ladder reaching to heaven with angels ascending and descending. God reaffirms His covenant with Jacob. Jacob works for Laban, marries Leah and Rachel, and fathers many children. Despite hardship and deceit, Jacob prospers and prepares to return to Canaan.

Hosea recalls Jacob's struggles with God and men, calling Israel to return to God with faithfulness, justice, and hope. Israel is reminded of God's past deliverance and His call to repentance.

Yeshua tells Nathanael he will see angels ascending and descending upon the Son of Man, directly linking Jacob's vision to Himself as the connection between heaven and earth.

CONNECTIONS

- Jacob's ladder symbolizes God's connection with His people, fulfilled in Yeshua.

- Hosea calls Israel to repentance, just as Jacob had to return to God.

- Messiah is the bridge between heaven and earth.

REFLECTION QUESTIONS

1. What does Jacob's ladder reveal about God's presence in my life?

2. How do I respond to God's call to return in faithfulness?

3. What does it mean for Yeshua to be the ladder between heaven and earth?

4. How can I find hope in God's covenant even during hardship?

VAYISHLACH 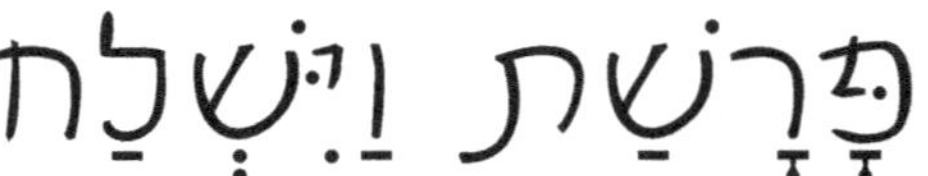

Jacob prepares to meet Esau, sending gifts ahead and praying for protection. That night he wrestles with a mysterious man and receives the name Israel. Esau surprisingly welcomes Jacob peacefully. Later, Jacob's family faces troubles, including the violation of Dinah and the violent response of Simeon and Levi. Jacob returns to Bethel and the covenant promises are reaffirmed.

Obadiah prophesies judgment against Edom, descendants of Esau, for their pride and violence against Israel. Yet God promises deliverance and the establishment of His kingdom.

Yeshua, in Gethsemane, wrestles in prayer before His arrest, submitting to the Father's will. His struggle reflects Jacob's wrestling, showing surrender and perseverance in God's plan.

CONNECTIONS

- Jacob and Esau's reconciliation contrasts with Edom's later hostility in Obadiah.

- Wrestling with God: Jacob physically, Yeshua spiritually in Gethsemane.

- God's promises are reaffirmed even through conflict.

REFLECTION QUESTIONS

1. What does Jacob's wrestling teach me about perseverance in prayer?

2. How do I reconcile with those I fear or have wronged?

3. What does Obadiah's prophecy show me about pride and humility?

4. How does Yeshua's surrender in Gethsemane shape my own obedience?

VAYESHEV

TORAH: GENESIS 37:1–40:23
HAFTARA: AMOS 2:6–3:8
NEW TESTAMENT: ACTS 7:9–16

Joseph, Jacob's favored son, is hated by his brothers who sell him into slavery. Joseph rises
in Potiphar's house but is falsely accused and imprisoned. In prison, Joseph interprets dreams,
showing God's favor is still with him.

Amos condemns Israel for injustice, cruelty, and selling the righteous for silver. God
calls His people to account, affirming that He reveals His plans to His prophets.

Stephen recounts Joseph's story in Acts, showing how God used his
suffering and betrayal to preserve Israel and prepare the way for deliverance.

<u>CONNECTIONS</u>

- Joseph's betrayal mirrors Israel's injustices condemned in Amos.

- Joseph as a type of Messiah: rejected, yet chosen for deliverance.

- Stephen connects Joseph's story to God's unfolding plan of redemption.

REFLECTION QUESTIONS

1. How do I respond when others betray or reject me?

2. What injustices in my world reflect Amos' warning?

3. How does Joseph's story foreshadow Messiah's suffering and exaltation?

4. Where do I see God's hidden purposes in times of hardship?

MIKETZ

פָּרָשַׁת מִקֵּץ

TORAH: GENESIS 41:1-44:17
HAFTARA: 1 KINGS 3:15-4:1
NEW TESTAMENT: LUKE 4:14-30

Pharaoh dreams troubling dreams, and Joseph interprets them as seven years of
plenty followed by seven years of famine. Joseph is elevated to second in command of Egypt.
During the famine, Joseph's brothers come seeking food, not recognizing him. Joseph tests
them, beginning the process of reconciliation.

Solomon, newly king, prays for wisdom and receives it from God. His wisdom is
displayed in judging a case between two women. His rule begins with God-given
discernment.

Yeshua begins His ministry in Galilee, teaching in the synagogue with authority. He is rejected
by many who cannot accept His identity, echoing Joseph's rejection by his brothers.

CONNECTIONS

- Joseph's God-given wisdom parallels Solomon's gift of wisdom.

- Joseph's rejection foreshadows Messiah's rejection by His people.

- God raises deliverers in unexpected ways for His purposes.

REFLECTION QUESTIONS 39

1. How do I seek God's wisdom in decisions?

2. What can I learn from Joseph's humility and faithfulness in exile?

3. How do I respond when God raises up leaders I did not expect?

4. How do I apply Yeshua's example of faithful teaching despite rejection?

VAYIGASH

פָּרָשַׁת וַיִּגַּשׁ

TORAH: GENESIS 44:18–47:27
HAFTARA: EZEKIEL 37:15–28
NEW TESTAMENT: JOHN 10:1–18

Judah pleads with Joseph to take him as a slave instead of Benjamin, showing repentance and sacrificial love. Joseph reveals his identity to his brothers, forgives them, and declares God's hand in their survival. Jacob and his family move to Egypt, where they are given land in Goshen.

Ezekiel prophesies that Judah and Israel will be reunited into one kingdom under one shepherd. God promises to cleanse and restore His people forever.

Yeshua declares Himself the Good Shepherd who lays down His life for the sheep, uniting them into one flock under His care.

CONNECTIONS

- Judah's self-sacrifice foreshadows Messiah's ultimate sacrifice.

- Joseph as a shepherd of Israel connects to Ezekiel's prophecy.

- Yeshua fulfills the role of the Good Shepherd, uniting all God's people.

REFLECTION QUESTIONS

1. What does Judah's transformation teach me about repentance?

2. How do I see God's hand at work even in painful circumstances?

3. What does it mean that Yeshua is my Good Shepherd?

4. How do I participate in God's plan to unite His people?

VAYECHI

TORAH: GENESIS 47:28–50:26
HAFTARA: 1 KINGS 2:1–12
NEW TESTAMENT: HEBREWS 11:21–22

Jacob blesses his sons, prophesying their future tribes. He blesses Joseph's sons, Ephraim and Manasseh, giving the younger Ephraim the greater blessing. After Jacob's death, Joseph reassures his brothers of forgiveness, affirming God's sovereignty in using their actions for good. Joseph dies in Egypt, requesting his bones be carried back to the Promised Land.

David, near death, charges Solomon to be strong, walk in God's ways, and keep His commands, securing the kingdom's future.

Hebrews recalls Jacob blessing his sons and Joseph's faith in God's promises, highlighting their trust in God's covenant beyond their lifetimes.

CONNECTIONS

- Blessings for future generations: Jacob and David both prepare for transition.

- Faith in God's promises even when not yet fulfilled.

- Messiah as the ultimate King and Shepherd securing God's covenant.

REFLECTION QUESTIONS

1. What legacy of faith am I leaving for the next generation?

2. How do I trust God's promises beyond my lifetime?

3. What do Jacob's and Joseph's final words teach me about faith?

4. How does David's charge to Solomon inspire my own obedience?

SHEMOT

EXODUS

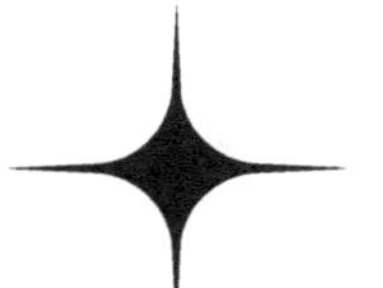

Shemot (Exodus) – "Names"

Introduction
Exodus is the story of God's redemption. Israel is delivered from slavery, receives Torah at Sinai, and is transformed into God's covenant nation. It is the story of liberation, covenant, and divine presence.

Historical Background
Traditionally, Moses is seen as the author, recording both Israel's history and the giving of Torah. Exodus became the theological anchor of Israel's festivals, especially Passover, shaping Jewish memory of God as Redeemer.

Modern Scholarship
Scholars often view Exodus as historical memory shaped into liturgy. Some argue the Exodus was a smaller-scale migration, later remembered as Israel's defining salvation. The Tabernacle sections are sometimes seen as reflecting later priestly traditions during the exile, emphasizing God's continued presence.

For Messianic believers, these perspectives highlight how God's saving acts — whether through mighty miracles or remembered liturgy — point ultimately to Yeshua, the true Passover Lamb and divine presence with His people.

SHEMOT

פָּרָשַׁת שְׁמוֹת

TORAH: EXODUS 1:1–6:1
HAFTARA: ISAIAH 27:6–28:13; 29:22–23
NEW TESTAMENT: MATTHEW 2:13–23

The descendants of Israel multiply in Egypt and are enslaved by Pharaoh. Moses is born, saved from death, raised in Pharaoh's household, and later flees to Midian after killing an Egyptian. God appears to Moses in the burning bush, calling him to deliver Israel. God assures Moses of His presence and reveals His name as the God of Abraham, Isaac, and Jacob.

Isaiah promises Israel's restoration, describing them as a fruitful vineyard. God's people will flourish again, and their iniquity will be removed through God's judgment and redemption.

Matthew recounts how Joseph and Mary flee to Egypt with Yeshua, fulfilling prophecy, and later return, echoing Israel's deliverance from Egypt.

CONNECTIONS

- God delivers His people from oppression in both Exodus and Isaiah.

- Moses' calling foreshadows Messiah's greater deliverance.

- Yeshua relives Israel's story, coming out of Egypt as the Redeemer.

REFLECTION QUESTIONS

1. How do I respond to God's call in my life, even when I feel unqualified?

2. Where do I see God delivering His people today?

3. What does God's covenant name reveal about His character?

4. How does Yeshua fulfill Israel's story in my faith?

VAERA

TORAH: EXODUS 6:2–9:35
HAFTARA: EZEKIEL 28:25–29:21
NEW TESTAMENT: ROMANS 9:17–33

God reaffirms His covenant to redeem Israel. Moses and Aaron confront Pharaoh, and God sends the first seven plagues upon Egypt, showing His power over Pharaoh and the Egyptian gods. Despite the signs, Pharaoh hardens his heart.

Ezekiel prophesies Egypt's downfall, showing that God alone is sovereign over nations and their rulers.

Paul cites Pharaoh as an example of God's sovereignty, using him to display His power and mercy, emphasizing salvation by faith rather than works.

CONNECTIONS

God's sovereignty over Pharaoh and Egypt is emphasized in all readings.

The plagues reveal God's power to redeem and judge.

Paul explains God's sovereignty in election and mercy through Pharaoh's example.

REFLECTION QUESTIONS

1. How does God's sovereignty give me confidence in difficult times?

2. What do the plagues reveal about God's power and justice?

3. How do I balance God's sovereignty and human responsibility?

4. How do I respond when my heart is tempted to harden?

פָּרָשַׁת בֹּא

TORAH: EXODUS 10:1–13:16
HAFTARA: JEREMIAH 46:13–28
NEW TESTAMENT: LUKE 22:7–20

God sends the final plagues, including darkness and the death of the firstborn. He commands Israel to celebrate Passover as a memorial of their deliverance. Pharaoh finally releases the Israelites, who depart Egypt with God's mighty hand displayed.

Jeremiah foretells God's judgment against Egypt and reassures Israel of His deliverance and covenant faithfulness.

Yeshua celebrates Passover with His disciples, instituting the Lord's Supper as a remembrance of His sacrifice as the true Passover Lamb.

CONNECTIONS

- Passover unites all readings: God's deliverance from Egypt, assurance in Jeremiah, and fulfillment in Messiah.

- The blood of the lamb in Exodus foreshadows Yeshua's sacrifice.

- God's covenant faithfulness assures redemption across generations.

REFLECTION QUESTIONS

1. How does remembering Passover strengthen my faith today?

2. What does the blood of the lamb mean for my life in Messiah?

3. How does Jeremiah's assurance of deliverance apply to me?

4. How do I prepare my heart to celebrate God's redemption?

BESHALACH

פָּרָשַׁת בְּשַׁלַּח

TORAH: EXODUS 13:17–17:16
HAFTARA: JUDGES 4:4–5:31
NEW TESTAMENT: REVELATION 15:1–4

Israel leaves Egypt and crosses the Red Sea, where God delivers them by parting the waters and drowning Pharaoh's army. Miriam leads the women in song. In the wilderness, the people complain about food and water, but God provides manna and water from a rock. Israel also defeats Amalek with Moses' hands lifted in prayer.

Deborah and Barak lead Israel to victory over Sisera, and Deborah sings a song of praise to God, echoing the song at the sea.

Revelation describes those redeemed singing the Song of Moses and the Song of the Lamb, celebrating God's ultimate victory over evil.

CONNECTIONS

- Songs of deliverance: Miriam, Deborah, and Revelation's redeemed.

- God provides for His people in the wilderness and in Messiah.

- Victory comes through God's power and intercession.

1. How does remembering Passover strengthen my faith today?

2. What does the blood of the lamb mean for my life in Messiah?

3. How does Jeremiah's assurance of deliverance apply to me?

4. How do I prepare my heart to celebrate God's redemption?

YITRO

פָּרָשַׁת יִתְרוֹ

TORAH: EXODUS 18:1–20:23
HAFTARA: ISAIAH 6:1–7:6; 9:5–6
NEW TESTAMENT: MATTHEW 5:1–20

Jethro advises Moses to appoint judges to share the burden of leadership. At Mount Sinai, God makes a covenant with Israel, giving them the Ten Commandments as the foundation of His law. The people tremble at God's presence and agree to obey His covenant.

Isaiah sees a vision of God's holiness, with angels crying 'Holy, holy, holy.' He is commissioned to speak God's word to Israel despite their hardness of heart. The promise of Immanuel gives hope of deliverance.

Yeshua, in the Sermon on the Mount, teaches the heart of God's law. He fulfills the Torah and calls His disciples to live in deeper righteousness.

CONNECTIONS

- The giving of the Torah at Sinai connects with Yeshua's teaching of Torah's fullness.

- Isaiah's vision of holiness reflects Sinai's awe-inspiring presence.

- God calls His people to covenant obedience in every generation.

1. How do I share leadership burdens like Moses did?

2. What does Sinai teach me about God's holiness?

3. How do I live out the spirit of the commandments in Messiah?

4. What does Yeshua mean when He says He came to fulfill the Torah?

____

MISHPATIM   פָּרָשַׁת מִשְׁפָּטִים

TORAH: EXODUS 21:1-24:18
HAFTARA: JEREMIAH 34:8-22; 33:25-26
NEW TESTAMENT: MATTHEW 17:1-9

This portion outlines civil and social laws, including justice, property rights, and care for the vulnerable. It emphasizes fairness, integrity, and compassion in society. The covenant is ratified at Sinai, with Moses sprinkling blood on the altar and the people. Moses ascends Mount Sinai for forty days.

Jeremiah condemns Judah for breaking their covenant by re-enslaving freed servants, showing disregard for God's commands. God warns of judgment but reaffirms His covenant with David.

At the Transfiguration, Yeshua appears with Moses and Elijah, affirming His fulfillment of the Law and the Prophets, as God's beloved Son.

<u>CONNECTIONS</u>

- God's covenant demands justice and compassion.

- Jeremiah exposes Israel's covenant failure; Yeshua fulfills it perfectly.

- The Transfiguration highlights Yeshua as the embodiment of Torah and prophecy.

REFLECTION QUESTIONS

1. How do I live out God's justice in my relationships?

2. What does covenant faithfulness look like today?

3. How does Yeshua fulfill the Law and the Prophets?

4. How do I encounter God's presence like Israel at Sinai or the disciples at the Transfiguration?

TERUMAH

פָּרָשַׁת תְּרוּמָה

TORAH: EXODUS 25:1–27:19
HAFTARA: 1 KINGS 5:26–6:13
NEW TESTAMENT: HEBREWS 9:1–28

God commands Israel to bring offerings for the building of the Tabernacle. Instructions are given for the Ark of the Covenant, the table, the lampstand, and the sanctuary structure. God promises to dwell among His people through this holy dwelling place.

Solomon builds the Temple in Jerusalem, fulfilling the vision of a permanent dwelling place for God's presence among His people.

Hebrews explains that Messiah entered the greater heavenly Tabernacle, offering His own blood once for all for eternal redemption.

CONNECTIONS

- The Tabernacle and Temple foreshadow Messiah's greater work.

- God dwells among His people in the wilderness, in the Temple, and through Messiah.

- Messiah's sacrifice surpasses the earthly Tabernacle.

REFLECTION QUESTIONS

1. How do I offer my best to God as Israel did for the Tabernacle?

2. What does God's dwelling presence mean in my life today?

3. How does Messiah fulfill the Tabernacle's purpose?

4. How can my community reflect God's holiness as His dwelling place?

TETZAVEH

פָּרָשַׁת תְּצַוֶּה

TORAH: EXODUS 27:20–30:10
HAFTARA: EZEKIEL 43:10–27
NEW TESTAMENT: REVELATION 1:9–20

God commands that pure olive oil be brought for the lamp. Instructions are given for priestly garments, consecration of Aaron and his sons, and the altar of incense. God establishes the priesthood to serve Him in holiness.

Ezekiel describes the future Temple and its altar, emphasizing God's holiness and the restoration of worship.

John sees Yeshua in a vision clothed as the High Priest, standing among the lampstands, shining with divine glory.

CONNECTIONS

- The priestly garments and service foreshadow Messiah as High Priest.

- Ezekiel's vision emphasizes holiness in worship.

- Yeshua is the true High Priest in the heavenly Temple.

REFLECTION QUESTIONS

1. What does the priesthood teach me about holiness and service?

2. How can I keep the light of God burning in my life?

3. How do I see Yeshua as my High Priest today?

4. What does it mean for the community to be a kingdom of priests?

KI TISA

פָּרָשַׁת כִּי תִשָּׂא

TORAH: EXODUS 30:11–34:35
HAFTARA: 1 KINGS 18:1–39
NEW TESTAMENT: 2 CORINTHIANS 3:1–18

Moses is given instructions for the census, the bronze basin, anointing oil, and the Sabbath. Israel sins by making a golden calf while Moses is on Mount Sinai. Moses intercedes, and God renews the covenant, revealing His merciful character. Moses' face shines after being in God's presence.

Elijah confronts the prophets of Baal on Mount Carmel. God answers with fire, proving He alone is God and calling Israel back to faithfulness.

Paul contrasts the fading glory of Moses' face with the surpassing glory of the Spirit in Messiah. Believers are transformed into God's image with ever-increasing glory.

CONNECTIONS

- Idolatry confronted: golden calf, Baal, and Paul's warning against veils.

- God's glory revealed on Sinai, Carmel, and in Messiah.

- Renewed covenant and Spirit-filled transformation.

REFLECTION QUESTIONS

1. Where am I tempted to rely on idols instead of God?

2. How do I see God's mercy after failure?

3. What does it mean to reflect God's glory in my life?

4. How can I walk in the Spirit's freedom more fully?

VAYAKHEL

פָּרָשַׁת וַיַּקְהֵל

TORAH: EXODUS 35:1–38:20
HAFTARA: 1 KINGS 7:40–50
NEW TESTAMENT: MATTHEW 12:1–13

Moses assembles the people and reminds them of the Sabbath. The people generously bring offerings for the Tabernacle. Skilled artisans build the furnishings as God commanded. The work is done with willing hearts and unity.

Solomon's craftsmen complete the furnishings of the Temple with great care, reflecting the glory of God's dwelling place.

Yeshua teaches that the Sabbath is made for life and mercy. He heals on the Sabbath, showing the true heart of God's command.

CONNECTIONS

- Generosity and skill used to build God's dwelling place.

- Temple and Tabernacle both reflect God's glory and presence.

- Messiah restores the true purpose of Sabbath and worship.

REFLECTION QUESTIONS

1. How do I contribute my gifts to God's dwelling place today?

2. What does generosity reveal about my heart toward God?

3. How do I honor Sabbath in spirit and truth?

4. What can I learn from the unity of Israel in building the Tabernacle?

PEKUDEI פָּרָשַׁת פְּקוּדֵי

The inventory of the Tabernacle is recorded, showing faithfulness in using the offerings. The Tabernacle is completed and erected. God's glory fills the sanctuary, and His presence leads Israel through the wilderness as a cloud by day and fire by night.

The Temple is completed, and the Ark is brought in. God's glory fills the Temple, affirming His presence among His people.

John sees the heavenly Temple opened, with God's glory revealed before final judgment. God's presence is central to His people's redemption.

CONNECTIONS

- God's glory fills the Tabernacle, Temple, and heavenly sanctuary.

- Faithful stewardship of offerings reflects covenant obedience.

- Messiah's presence ensures God's dwelling with His people forever.

REFLECTION QUESTIONS

1. How do I faithfully steward what God has entrusted to me?

2. What does it mean for God's glory to fill my life and community?

3. How do I live with awareness of God's constant presence?

4. How does Revelation's vision give me hope today?

VAYIKRA

LEVITICUS

Vayikra (Leviticus) – "And He Called"

Introduction

Leviticus is the manual of holiness, worship, and covenant life. It teaches how God's people can dwell in His presence through sacrifices, priesthood, and festivals.

Historical Background

Traditionally, Moses received these laws directly from God at Sinai. For centuries, Leviticus served as Israel's guide for sacrificial worship and priestly holiness.

Modern Scholarship

Modern research sees Leviticus as reflecting priestly traditions (the "P" source in documentary theory), likely shaped during or after the exile when the Temple was central to identity. The holiness code (Leviticus 17–26) may reflect an older core, emphasizing ethical holiness alongside ritual.

For Believers, Leviticus is not merely ritual instruction but a prophetic foreshadowing: sacrifices point to Yeshua's atonement, the High Priest anticipates His priesthood, and the festivals reveal God's redemptive calendar.

VAYIKRA פָּרָשַׁת וַיִּקְרָא

TORAH: LEVITICUS 1:1–5:26
HAFTARA: ISAIAH 43:21–44:23
NEW TESTAMENT: HEBREWS 10:1–18

God gives instructions for offerings: burnt, grain, peace, sin, and guilt offerings. These sacrifices provide atonement and restore fellowship between God and His people. The emphasis is on holiness and drawing near to God through obedience.

Isaiah contrasts God's faithfulness with Israel's sins. Despite their failures, God promises to blot out transgressions for His own sake and redeem His people.

Hebrews explains that Messiah's sacrifice fulfills the sacrificial system once for all, making further sacrifices unnecessary. His offering perfects believers forever.

CONNECTIONS

- Sacrifices in Torah point to Messiah's ultimate sacrifice.

- Isaiah highlights forgiveness and redemption despite sin.

- Messiah fulfills and surpasses the Levitical system.

REFLECTION QUESTIONS

1. How do I understand the seriousness of sin and atonement?

2. What does God's promise of forgiveness mean for me today?

3. How do I live in the freedom of Messiah's perfect sacrifice?

4. How do I show gratitude for redemption in my daily walk?

TZAV

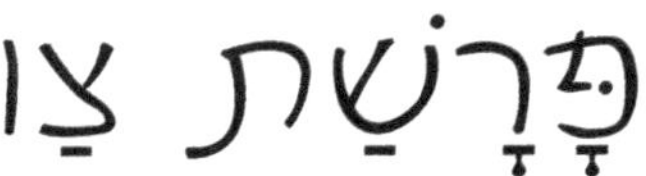

TORAH: LEVITICUS 6:1-8:36
HAFTARA: JEREMIAH 7:21-8:3; 9:22-23
NEW TESTAMENT: MARK 12:28-24

Tzav continues the laws of the offerings, including the burnt offering, grain offering, sin offering, and guilt offering. The priestly duties are detailed, emphasizing holiness and obedience in service. The consecration of Aaron and his sons is described, marking the beginning of their priestly ministry.

Jeremiah rebukes Israel for offering sacrifices without true obedience. God desires justice, mercy, and faithfulness rather than empty ritual.

Yeshua teaches the greatest commandments: to love God with all one's heart, soul, mind, and strength, and to love one's neighbor as oneself. He affirms that these embody the heart of Torah.

CONNECTIONS

- Sacrifices in Torah reveal the seriousness of sin and the holiness of God.

- Jeremiah warns against relying on ritual without obedience, echoing the Torah's call for holiness.

- Yeshua identifies love of God and neighbor as the essence of all the commandments

REFLECTION QUESTIONS

1. What does Tzav teach me about holiness and God's presence?

2. How do Jeremiah's words challenge my own worship and obedience?

3. How does Yeshua connect the Torah's commandments to love?

4. What areas of my life need deeper devotion to God and neighbor?

SHMINI

פָּרָשַׁת שְׁמִינִי

TORAH: LEVITICUS 9:1–11:47
HAFTARA: 2 SAMUEL 6:1–7:17
NEW TESTAMENT: ACTS 10:1–35

On the eighth day, Aaron and his sons begin their priestly service. Fire from God consumes the offering, but Nadab and Abihu die for offering unauthorized fire. Laws of clean and unclean foods are given, teaching holiness and distinction.

David brings the Ark to Jerusalem, but Uzzah dies when he touches it irreverently. Later, the Ark is brought with joy, showing the seriousness of God's holiness.

Peter receives a vision of clean and unclean animals, teaching that God has made Gentiles clean through Messiah. The gospel is for all nations without partiality.

CONNECTIONS

- God's holiness demands reverence: Nadab, Uzzah, and Peter's vision.

- Clean and unclean laws point to separation for God's purposes.

- Messiah unites Jew and Gentile into one holy people.

REFLECTION QUESTIONS

1. What do Nadab and Abihu's deaths teach me about reverence for God?

2. How do I live distinctly as one set apart for God?

3. What does Peter's vision teach me about God's inclusion of the nations?

4. How do I honor God's holiness in my worship and daily life?

TAZRIA

פָּרָשַׁת תַזְרִיעַ

TORAH: LEVITICUS 12:1–13:59
HAFTARA: 2 KINGS 4:42–5:19
NEW TESTAMENT: MARK 1:40–45

This portion addresses purification after childbirth and laws regarding leprosy (tzara'at). Priests inspect skin diseases and quarantine the afflicted. The emphasis is on holiness and separation from impurity.

Naaman, a Syrian commander, is healed of leprosy by following Elisha's instructions to wash in the Jordan River. God's power extends beyond Israel, showing His mercy to the nations.

Yeshua heals a man with leprosy, showing His authority to cleanse and His compassion. Unlike the priests who could only declare clean, Yeshua makes clean by His word.

CONNECTIONS

- Laws of purity foreshadow Messiah's healing power.

- Naaman's cleansing shows God's mercy to the nations.

- Yeshua fulfills the Torah by cleansing the unclean.

REFLECTION QUESTIONS

1. What does biblical leprosy teach me about sin and separation?

2. How does Naaman's humility challenge my faith?

3. What does Yeshua's touch teach me about His compassion?

4. How do I bring my impurities to Messiah for cleansing?

METZORA

פָּרָשַׁת מְצֹרָע

TORAH: LEVITICUS 14:1–15:33
HAFTARA: 2 KINGS 7:3–20
NEW TESTAMENT: LUKE 17:11–19

This portion explains the purification rituals for those healed of leprosy and for houses affected by it. Sacrifices and washings restore people to the community. Laws of bodily discharges emphasize holiness in all aspects of life.

Four lepers bring good news of deliverance to Samaria during a famine, fulfilling God's word through Elisha. Their condition becomes the means of blessing for others.

Yeshua heals ten lepers, but only one, a Samaritan, returns to give thanks. His gratitude highlights faith and recognition of God's mercy.

CONNECTIONS

- Purification and restoration to the community.

- God uses lepers in 2 Kings to bring salvation news.

- Messiah brings ultimate cleansing and calls for gratitude.

1. What does restoration to community mean in my spiritual walk?

2. How do I respond with gratitude like the Samaritan leper?

3. Where have I seen God use unlikely people to bring good news?

4. What does holiness look like in every aspect of my life?

ACHAREI MOT פָּרָשַׁת אַחֲרֵי מוֹת

TORAH: LEVITICUS 16:1–18:30
HAFTARA: EZEKIEL 22:1–19
NEW TESTAMENT: HEBREWS 9:11–28

God gives instructions for Yom Kippur, the Day of Atonement. The High Priest enters the Holy of Holies with sacrifices for himself and the people, and the scapegoat carries away Israel's sins. The portion also prohibits idolatry, improper sacrifices, and sexual immorality.

Ezekiel condemns Jerusalem's sins, including bloodshed and idolatry, warning of God's judgment for their impurity.

Hebrews explains that Messiah, as High Priest, entered the greater heavenly sanctuary with His own blood, providing eternal redemption.

CONNECTIONS

- Yom Kippur foreshadows Messiah's atoning sacrifice.

- Israel's sins in Ezekiel mirror the need for cleansing and atonement.

- Messiah fulfills Yom Kippur in the heavenly Holy of Holies.

REFLECTION QUESTIONS

1. How does the scapegoat picture Messiah's work for me?

2. What does Yom Kippur teach me about holiness and repentance?

3. How do I live in the reality of Messiah's eternal redemption?

4. Where do I need to repent of idolatry or impurity?

KEDOSHIM

פָּרָשַׁת קְדֹשִׁים

TORAH: LEVITICUS 19:1–20:27
HAFTARA: AMOS 9:7–15
NEW TESTAMENT: 1 PETER 1:13–25

God commands Israel to be holy as He is holy. Laws include honoring parents, honesty, justice, sexual purity, love for neighbor, and separation from pagan practices. The emphasis is on reflecting God's holiness in everyday life.

Amos speaks of God's judgment on sinful nations but promises restoration for Israel. God's covenant people will be planted securely in their land.

Peter exhorts believers to live holy lives, redeemed by Messiah's blood. Holiness is expressed through obedience, love, and reverence for God.

<u>CONNECTIONS</u>

- Holiness is God's standard in Torah, Prophets, and NT.

- Love for neighbor is central to Torah and fulfilled in Messiah.

- God's covenant promises restoration for His holy people.

REFLECTION QUESTIONS

1. What does it mean for me to be holy as God is holy?

2. How do I live out love for my neighbor in practical ways?

3. How does Messiah's blood motivate my holiness?

4. What promises of restoration give me hope?

EMOR

TORAH: LEVITICUS 21:1–24:23
HAFTARA: EZEKIEL 44:15–31
NEW TESTAMENT: LUKE 18:1–30

God gives laws for priests regarding purity and holiness. Instructions for appointed feasts—Passover, Shavuot, Yom Kippur, and Sukkot—are detailed. Rules about the menorah and showbread emphasize continual devotion. Penalties for blasphemy and justice are given.

Ezekiel describes the priestly duties in the future Temple, emphasizing holiness and separation from uncleanness.

Yeshua teaches persistence in prayer and warns about wealth. He affirms eternal rewards for those who follow Him wholeheartedly.

CONNECTIONS

- Priestly holiness and festival observances tie Torah and Ezekiel together.

- Messiah teaches about devotion, sacrifice, and eternal reward.

- God calls His people to continual holiness and worship.

REFLECTION QUESTIONS

1. How do I practice holiness in worship and daily life?

2. What do the biblical feasts teach me about God's plan of redemption?

3. How do I persist in prayer as Yeshua taught?

4. What does it mean to value eternal reward above earthly wealth?

BEHAR

פָּרָשַׁת בְּהַר

TORAH: LEVITICUS 25:1–26:2
HAFTARA: JEREMIAH 32:6–27
NEW TESTAMENT: LUKE 4:16–21

God commands the Sabbatical year (Shmita) and the Jubilee year (Yovel), during which the land rests and property is restored. These laws emphasize trust in God's provision, justice, and compassion for the poor.

Jeremiah, while imprisoned, buys a field as a prophetic act of hope that God will restore Israel to their land despite exile.

Yeshua reads from Isaiah in the synagogue, proclaiming the year of the Lord's favor, echoing Jubilee themes of release and restoration.

CONNECTIONS

- Jubilee laws foreshadow Messiah's proclamation of freedom.

- Jeremiah's act of faith parallels God's promise of restoration.

- Yeshua fulfills the Jubilee in His ministry of release and redemption.

REFLECTION QUESTIONS

1. How do I practice trust in God's provision?

2. What does Jubilee teach me about justice and restoration?

3. How does Yeshua fulfill the year of the Lord's favor in my life?

4. How can I live generously and release others as God commands?

BECHUKOTAI פָּרָשַׁת בְּחֻקֹּתַי

TORAH: LEVITICUS 26:3–27:34
HAFTARA: JEREMIAH 16:19–17:14
NEW TESTAMENT: MATTHEW 22:1–14

God promises blessings for obedience, including peace, prosperity, and His presence. Disobedience brings curses, exile, and desolation. Yet God promises He will remember His covenant and not abandon Israel. Instructions for vows and dedications are given.

Jeremiah warns against trusting in human strength instead of God. He describes blessings for those who trust in the Lord and curses for those who turn away.

Yeshua teaches the parable of the wedding banquet, showing that many are invited but only those prepared and faithful will share in the blessing.

CONNECTIONS

- Blessings and curses emphasize covenant responsibility.

- Trust in God is central in Torah, Prophets, and Messiah's teaching.

- God's covenant faithfulness remains despite disobedience.

REFLECTION QUESTIONS

1. What blessings have I experienced from walking in obedience?

2. Where am I tempted to trust in my own strength instead of God?

3. What does Messiah's parable teach me about readiness for God's kingdom?

4. How do I live in hope of God's covenant faithfulness even when I fail?

✦BAMIDBAR✦

NUMBERS

Bamidbar (Numbers) – "In the Wilderness"

Introduction
Numbers recounts Israel's wilderness journey, marked by testing, rebellion, and God's faithfulness. It shows that even in failure, God's covenant purposes remain.

Historical Background
Tradition credits Moses with recording events during Israel's wanderings. The censuses and camp arrangements reveal Israel's structure as a covenant nation.

Modern Scholarship
Scholars see Numbers as a composite narrative blending historical memory and priestly editing. Some sections (like Balaam's oracles) may preserve ancient poetic traditions, while census lists reflect later priestly organization.

For believers, Numbers teaches that God's faithfulness outlasts human failure. Messiah is revealed in the intercession of Moses, the water from the rock, and the bronze serpent lifted up.

BAMIDBAR פָּרָשַׁת בְּמִדְבַּר

God commands a census of Israel's tribes and organizes the camp around the Tabernacle. The Levites are set apart for service, caring for the sanctuary and assisting the priests. The structure emphasizes God's order and holiness among His people.

Hosea speaks of Israel as God's unfaithful wife but promises restoration and renewed covenant love. God will betroth His people to Himself forever.

Luke describes the census during Yeshua's birth, linking Israel's history with God's ultimate redemption. Simeon proclaims Yeshua as salvation for Israel and a light to the nations.

CONNECTIONS

- Census and order in Torah connect with Luke's account of Yeshua's birth.

- Hosea highlights God's covenant love and restoration.

- Messiah fulfills God's plan to dwell among His people.

REFLECTION QUESTIONS

1. How do I see God's order and holiness shaping my community?

2. Where have I experienced God's covenant love despite failure?

3. What does it mean that Yeshua is a light to the nations?

4. How do I dedicate myself to serving God like the Levites?

NASSO

פָּרָשַׁת נָשֹׂא

TORAH: NUMBERS 4:21–7:89
HAFTARA: JUDGES 13:2–25
NEW TESTAMENT: ACTS 21:17–26

This portion covers the duties of the Levites, laws of purity, restitution, the Sotah ritual, and the Nazirite vow. The priestly blessing is given: 'The Lord bless you and keep you…' The portion concludes with the leaders' offerings for the dedication of the Tabernacle.

The angel announces Samson's birth to his barren mother, setting him apart as a Nazirite from birth, showing God's calling and empowerment.

Paul participates in purification rites in Jerusalem, showing respect for Torah while following Messiah. His actions connect to vows and holiness practices.

CONNECTIONS

- Nazirite vow connects Torah, Samson, and Paul's example.

- The priestly blessing expresses God's covenant love.

- Holiness and dedication to God are central themes across all readings.

REFLECTION QUESTIONS

1. What does the priestly blessing mean for me today?

2. How do vows and commitments shape my walk with God?

3. What does Samson's calling teach me about God's empowerment?

4. How can I live a life set apart for God like the Nazirites?

BEHA'ALOTECHA   פָּרָשַׁת בְּהַעֲלֹתְךָ

TORAH: NUMBERS 8:1-12:16
HAFTARA: ZECHARIAH 2:14-4:7
NEW TESTAMENT: REVELATION 11:1-19

The menorah is set up, Levites are consecrated, and Passover is celebrated. God leads Israel with a cloud by day and fire by night. The people complain about food, and God provides quail but also judgment. Miriam and Aaron oppose Moses, and Miriam is struck with leprosy but later healed after Moses intercedes.

Zechariah sees visions of God's presence among His people, including the lampstand and olive trees symbolizing God's Spirit. God promises victory 'not by might nor by power, but by My Spirit.'

Revelation describes God's two witnesses, lampstands empowered by His Spirit, proclaiming truth with boldness before God's final victory.

CONNECTIONS

- Lampstands symbolize God's Spirit in Torah, Prophets, and NT.

- Moses' intercession shows Messiah's heart of mercy and prayer.

- God provides guidance and presence through His Spirit.

REFLECTION QUESTIONS

1. How do I rely on God's Spirit rather than my own strength?

2. What does the menorah symbolize for my faith community today?

3. How can I intercede like Moses for those in need of mercy?

4. How do I see God's presence leading me day by day?

SH'LACH

פָּרָשַׁת שְׁלַח־לְךָ

TORAH: NUMBERS 13:1–15:41
HAFTARA: JOSHUA 2:1-24
NEW TESTAMENT: HEBREWS 3:7-19

Twelve spies are sent to scout the land of Canaan. Ten return with a discouraging report, while Joshua and Caleb trust God's promise. The people rebel, leading to forty years of wandering. The portion ends with laws of offerings, Sabbath observance, and the command to wear tzitzit as reminders of God's commandments.

Rahab hides the Israelite spies in Jericho, declaring her faith in Israel's God. Her courage ensures deliverance for her family.

Hebrews warns believers not to harden their hearts as Israel did in the wilderness, but to trust God's promises with faith like Joshua and Caleb.

<u>CONNECTIONS</u>

- Spies' faith vs. fear parallels Israel's entry into the land.

- Rahab's faith contrasts with Israel's unbelief.

- Messiah calls us to steadfast trust in God's promises.

REFLECTION QUESTIONS

1. Do I respond with faith or fear to God's promises?

2. What does Rahab teach me about courage and faith?

3. How do tzitzit help remind me of God's commands today?

4. Where do I need to guard my heart against unbelief?

KORACH

פָּרָשַׁת קֹרַח

Korach and his followers rebel against Moses and Aaron, challenging their leadership. God judges the rebels, causing the earth to swallow them. Aaron's priesthood is confirmed when his staff buds. Laws are given concerning priestly duties and tithes.

Samuel rebukes Israel for rejecting God's kingship by asking for a human king. He reminds them of God's faithfulness and calls them to serve the Lord wholeheartedly.

Jude warns against false teachers, comparing them to Korach's rebellion, urging believers to contend for the faith with humility and truth.

CONNECTIONS

- Rebellion against God's chosen leaders is a recurring theme.

- Samuel warns Israel, echoing Korach's rebellion against authority.

- Messiah calls His followers to humility and faithfulness, not rebellion.

REFLECTION QUESTIONS

1. How do I respond to God's chosen leaders?

2. What does Korach's downfall teach me about pride?

3. Where do I see rebellion against God's authority today?

4. How can I remain faithful and humble in God's service?

CHUKAT

פָּרָשַׁת חֻקַּת

TORAH: NUMBERS 19:1–22:1
HAFTARA: JUDGES 11:1–33
NEW TESTAMENT: JOHN 3:1–21

God gives the laws of the red heifer for purification. Miriam dies, and the people complain about lack of water. Moses strikes the rock instead of speaking to it, leading to his exclusion from entering the land. Israel faces battles, including victory over Sihon and Og.

Jephthah delivers Israel from the Ammonites but makes a tragic vow. Despite his flaws, God uses him to save His people.

Yeshua teaches Nicodemus about being born again. He compares His crucifixion to Moses lifting up the bronze serpent for healing, pointing to salvation through faith in Him.

CONNECTIONS

- Water and life: Moses striking the rock, Jephthah's vow, Messiah's living water.

- Red heifer and bronze serpent both foreshadow Messiah's atonement.

- Faith in God's provision is central in all readings.

"

REFLECTION QUESTIONS

1. What does Moses' mistake teach me about obedience and holiness?

2. How does the red heifer foreshadow Messiah's sacrifice?

3. What does it mean to be born again in Messiah?

4. How do I respond to trials with faith rather than complaint?

BALAK

פָּרָשַׁת בָּלָק

TORAH: NUMBERS 22:2–25:9
HAFTARA: MICAH 5:6–6:8
NEW TESTAMENT: 2 PETER 2:1–22

Balak, king of Moab, hires Balaam to curse Israel, but God causes him to bless them instead. Balaam's donkey speaks, showing God's sovereignty. Balaam prophesies Israel's future victory, but Israel falls into sin with Moabite women and idolatry at Baal Peor.

Micah reminds Israel of God's saving acts and calls them to act justly, love mercy, and walk humbly with God.

Peter warns against false teachers like Balaam, motivated by greed and leading others astray. Believers are urged to live holy lives.

CONNECTIONS

- God's sovereignty over Balaam parallels His call to justice in Micah.

- False teachers are compared to Balaam in both Torah and NT.

- Holiness and humility are the antidote to idolatry and greed.

REFLECTION QUESTIONS

1. How do I discern true vs. false spiritual voices today?

2. What does Balaam's story teach me about God's sovereignty?

3. Where am I tempted by compromise with the world?

4. How can I live out Micah's call to justice, mercy, and humility?

PINCHAS

TORAH: NUMBERS 25:10–30:1
HAFTARA: 1 KINGS 18:46–19:21
NEW TESTAMENT: MATTHEW 26:1–13

Phinehas (Pinchas) zealously defends God's holiness by stopping a plague through his bold action. God makes a covenant of peace with him. The portion also includes a new census, laws of inheritance, and the appointment of Joshua as Moses' successor. Sacrificial offerings for the festivals are given.

Elijah flees from Jezebel after confronting the prophets of Baal. God meets him not in wind, earthquake, or fire, but in a gentle whisper, reaffirming His mission.

Yeshua is anointed by a woman in Bethany, preparing Him for burial. Her act of devotion contrasts with betrayal and indifference.

CONNECTIONS

- Zeal for God's holiness: Pinchas, Elijah, and Messiah's devotion.

- Leadership transitions: Moses to Joshua, Elijah to Elisha, fulfilled in Messiah.

- Devotion and faithfulness contrast with compromise and betrayal.

REFLECTION QUESTIONS

1. What does Pinchas' zeal teach me about standing for God's holiness?

2. How does Elijah's encounter with God encourage me in discouragement?

3. What does the woman's devotion to Yeshua teach me about worship?

4. How do I prepare myself to serve God faithfully like Joshua?

MATOT

פָּרָשַׁת מַטּוֹת

TORAH: NUMBERS 30:2–32:42
HAFTARA: JEREMIAH 1:1–2:3
NEW TESTAMENT: MATTHEW 5:33–37

Laws concerning vows are given, emphasizing faithfulness to one's word. Israel wages war against Midian, and the spoils are divided. The tribes of Reuben, Gad, and half of Manasseh request to settle east of the Jordan, agreeing to help conquer the land first.

Jeremiah is called as a prophet to Israel. God reassures him of His presence and declares His covenant love, recalling Israel's early devotion.

Yeshua teaches about oaths, urging His followers to let their 'Yes' be 'Yes' and their 'No,' 'No,' living with honesty and integrity.

CONNECTIONS

- Faithfulness to vows and God's covenant.

- God calls Jeremiah to faithfulness despite opposition.

- Messiah calls for integrity and truth in speech.

REFLECTION QUESTIONS

1. How do I honor my word in daily life?

2. What does Jeremiah's calling teach me about God's presence in my mission?

3. How do I practice integrity in my commitments?

4. Where is God calling me to courageous obedience?

MASEI

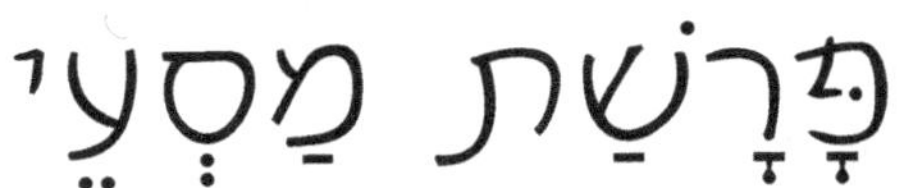

TORAH: NUMBERS 33:1–36:13
HAFTARA: JEREMIAH 2:4–28; 3:4
NEW TESTAMENT: JAMES 4:1–12

Israel's journeys are listed from Egypt to the plains of Moab. Instructions are given for dividing the land, appointing cities of refuge, and inheritance laws. The daughters of Zelophehad are again affirmed in their right to inheritance within their tribe.

God rebukes Israel for forsaking Him and turning to idols, describing their unfaithfulness like an adulterous spouse. Yet He calls them to return to Him.

James warns against quarrels, pride, and speaking against others, urging humility before God and submission to His will.

CONNECTIONS

- Israel's journeys remind believers of God's faithfulness.

- Idolatry and unfaithfulness are warned against in Torah and Prophets.

- NT emphasizes humility and submission to God's will.

REFLECTION QUESTIONS

1. What milestones in my journey show God's faithfulness?

2. How do I guard against idolatry in my life?

3. What does humility before God look like for me?

4. How do I trust God's justice like the daughters of Zelophehad?

DEVARIM

DEUTERONOMY

<h1 align="center"><u>Devarim (Deuteronomy) – "Words"</u></h1>

<u>Introduction</u>

Deuteronomy is Moses' final address, urging Israel to love and obey God. It renews the covenant and sets Israel on the threshold of the Land. Its central theme is covenant loyalty.

<u>Historical Background</u>

Tradition holds Moses delivered these speeches before his death, with Joshua completing the final verses. Deuteronomy shaped Israel's faith, and its rediscovery in Josiah's day (2 Kings 22) sparked revival.

<u>Modern Scholarship</u>

Scholars often see Deuteronomy as reflecting covenant treaty forms from the Ancient Near East. Many argue its core was written or compiled during Josiah's reforms (7th century BCE) to centralize worship in Jerusalem. Later editing may have occurred during the exile.

For Believers, this context highlights how God used covenant renewal to prepare Israel for Messiah. Yeshua quoted Deuteronomy in His wilderness temptation, showing its enduring authority.

DEVARIM

פָּרָשַׁת דְּבָרִים

Moses begins his final speeches, recounting Israel's journey from Sinai to the edge of the Promised Land. He recalls the appointment of leaders, the spies' rebellion, and victories over kings Sihon and Og. He encourages Israel to trust God as they enter the land.

Isaiah rebukes Judah for rebellion and empty worship, calling them to repentance and justice. God promises restoration for the repentant.

Yeshua foretells the destruction of the Temple and warns His disciples to remain steadfast through trials and tribulations before His return.

CONNECTIONS

- Moses and Isaiah both call Israel to remember and repent.

- God's judgment and restoration appear in both Torah and Prophets.

- Messiah calls His followers to endurance and faithfulness.

REFLECTION QUESTIONS

1. What lessons from my past journey strengthen my faith today?

2. Where do I need to repent and return to God?

3. How does Yeshua's warning prepare me for trials?

4. What does God's promise of restoration mean for me personally?

VAETCHANAN

פָּרָשַׁת וָאֶתְחַנַּן

Moses pleads to enter the land but is denied. He repeats the Ten Commandments and the Shema, calling Israel to love God wholeheartedly and obey His commandments. Israel is reminded of God's greatness and chosen covenant relationship.

Isaiah comforts Israel with the promise of God's redemption and incomparable power. God is sovereign over creation and tender toward His people.

Yeshua laments over Jerusalem's hardness of heart, longing to gather them as a hen gathers her chicks, but they refuse. He warns of judgment yet hints at restoration.

CONNECTIONS

- The Shema calls for wholehearted devotion to God.

- Isaiah and Yeshua both call Israel to recognize God's greatness.

- Moses, Isaiah, and Yeshua emphasize God's covenant faithfulness.

REFLECTION QUESTIONS

1. How do I live out the Shema in daily practice?

2. What does it mean to love God with all my heart, soul, and strength?

3. How do I find comfort in God's greatness?

4. What does Yeshua's lament teach me about God's heart for His people?

EIKEV

TORAH: DEUTERONOMY 7:12–11:25
HAFTARA: ISAIAH 49:14–51:3
NEW TESTAMENT: MATTHEW 4:1–11

Moses urges Israel to obey God's commands for blessing in the land. He reminds them of God's provision in the wilderness, including manna. He warns against pride and forgetting God. Obedience will bring victory and strength in the land.

Isaiah encourages Israel that though they feel forgotten, God has not abandoned them. He promises comfort, restoration, and justice.

Yeshua resists Satan's temptations in the wilderness by quoting Deuteronomy, showing perfect obedience to God's Word.

CONNECTIONS

- Obedience brings blessing: Moses, Isaiah, and Yeshua affirm this.

- Wilderness testing teaches reliance on God alone.

- God's promises of comfort and restoration sustain His people.

REFLECTION QUESTIONS

1. What blessings have I experienced through obedience?

2. Where am I tempted to forget God's provision?

3. How does Yeshua's example strengthen me in temptation?

4. What promises of restoration give me hope?

TORAH: DEUTERONOMY 11:26–16:17
HAFTARA: ISAIAH 54:11–55:5
NEW TESTAMENT: JOHN 6:35–51

Moses sets before Israel the blessing and the curse, depending on obedience or disobedience. Instructions are given for centralized worship, rejecting idolatry, dietary laws, tithes, care for the poor, and celebration of the festivals of Pesach, Shavuot, and Sukkot.

Isaiah proclaims God's everlasting covenant and invitation to the thirsty to come and drink freely, promising restoration and blessing for Israel.

Yeshua declares Himself the Bread of Life, the true provision from heaven, offering eternal life to all who believe in Him.

CONNECTIONS

- Choice of blessing or curse is echoed in Messiah's call to faith.

- God's covenant promises of provision are fulfilled in Yeshua.

- Festivals foreshadow Messiah as the Bread of Life and Redeemer.

REFLECTION QUESTIONS

. What choices am I making daily that lead to blessing or curse?

2. How do I care for the poor and needy as God commands?

3. What do the biblical festivals teach me about Messiah?

4. How do I experience Yeshua as the Bread of Life in my walk?

SHOFTIM

פָּרָשַׁת שׁוֹפְטִים

TORAH: DEUTERONOMY 11:26–16:17
HAFTARA: ISAIAH 54:11–55:5
NEW TESTAMENT: JOHN 6:35–51

Moses commands the appointment of judges, kings, priests, and prophets, emphasizing justice and fairness. The laws establish guidelines for leadership, warfare, and unsolved murders, with a focus on holiness and justice.

Isaiah comforts Israel with God's deliverance and sovereignty, promising redemption and restoration for His people.

Yeshua promises the Holy Spirit, the Counselor, who will guide believers into truth and righteousness.

CONNECTIONS

- Justice and righteousness are central themes in Torah and Prophets.

- Messiah provides the Spirit to guide His people into justice and truth.

- God calls His people to live in holiness under His leadership.

REFLECTION QUESTIONS

1. How do I live out God's call to justice and fairness?

2. What qualities of leadership does God value most?

3. How do I rely on the Holy Spirit to guide me into truth?

4. What does Isaiah's promise of deliverance mean for me today?

KI TETZEI

פָּרָשַׁת כִּי־תֵצֵא

This portion gives a wide range of laws covering family, morality, justice, warfare, and compassion. Key commands include returning lost property, fair treatment of workers, and remembering Amalek's attack. The emphasis is on practical holiness in everyday life.

Isaiah assures Israel of God's enduring love, comparing it to the days of Noah. Though they have suffered, God's covenant of peace will not be removed.

New Testament: Yeshua deepens the commandments about adultery and lust, teaching purity of heart and radical obedience to God's commands.

CONNECTIONS

- Practical holiness is expressed in daily obedience to God's commands.

- God's covenant of love sustains His people despite their failures.

- Messiah calls for purity of heart in obedience to God's Word.

REFLECTION QUESTIONS

1. What does it mean for me to live out holiness in daily actions?

2. How do I show compassion and justice to others?

3. Where do I need to pursue purity of heart?

4. What does God's covenant of peace mean for me today?

KI TAVO

פָּרָשַׁת כִּי־תָבוֹא

TORAH: DEUTERONOMY 21:10-25:19
HAFTARA: ISAIAH 54:1-10
NEW TESTAMENT: MATTHEW 5:27-30

Moses instructs Israel on bringing firstfruits and tithes, declaring God's faithfulness. Blessings and curses are proclaimed, showing the consequences of obedience or disobedience. Israel is reminded of God's deliverance and covenant at Moab.

Isaiah envisions Israel's future glory as a light to the nations. God's presence will bring everlasting peace and joy to His people.

Luke describes Yeshua's crucifixion and burial, showing Him as the suffering servant who brings redemption through His death.

CONNECTIONS

- Firstfruits offerings express gratitude for God's provision.

- Blessings and curses highlight covenant accountability.

- Messiah's suffering secures ultimate redemption and restoration.

REFLECTION QUESTIONS

1. How do I practice gratitude for God's blessings?

2. What does it mean to be a light to the nations today?

3. How does Messiah's suffering shape my view of obedience?

4. What choices am I making that lead to blessing or curse?

NITZAVIM

פָּרָשַׁת נִצָּבִים

TORAH: DEUTERONOMY 29:9–30:20
HAFTARA: ISAIAH 61:10–63:9
NEW TESTAMENT: ROMANS 10:1–13

Moses calls Israel to stand together and renew the covenant. He emphasizes God's command is not distant but very near, in their mouths and hearts. He sets before them life and death, blessing and curse, urging them to choose life by loving and obeying God.

Isaiah rejoices in God's salvation and describes the day of the Lord's vengeance and redemption. God's love and mercy toward His people are highlighted.

Paul quotes this passage, teaching that salvation is near, accessible to all who confess Yeshua as Lord and believe in His resurrection.

CONNECTIONS

- Choice of life and death, blessing and curse, is echoed by Paul's call to faith.

- Isaiah highlights God's redeeming love, fulfilled in Messiah.

- Messiah brings God's Word near, in our hearts and mouths.

REFLECTION QUESTIONS

1. What does it mean for me to choose life daily?

2. How do I keep God's Word near to my heart and lips?

3. What does Isaiah's vision of redemption teach me about God's love?

4. How does Paul connect Torah's message to Messiah's salvation?

VAYELECH 

TORAH: DEUTERONOMY 31:1–30
HAFTARA: HOSEA 14:2–10; MICAH 7:18–20
NEW TESTAMENT: HEBREWS 13:1–17

Moses prepares for his death, commissioning Joshua as his successor. God commands the reading of the Torah every seven years at Sukkot. God warns Israel of future unfaithfulness but promises His presence will not leave them.

Hosea calls Israel to repentance and promises God's healing and love. Micah emphasizes God's compassion and forgiveness, casting sins into the depths of the sea.

Hebrews urges believers to live in faithfulness, showing hospitality, honoring marriage, and trusting in God's presence. Messiah is the same yesterday, today, and forever.

CONNECTIONS

- Leadership transition from Moses to Joshua, echoed in Messiah's eternal leadership.

- Repentance and forgiveness are central themes in Torah, Prophets, and NT.

- God's presence is assured across generations.

REFLECTION QUESTIONS

1. What does Moses' commissioning of Joshua teach me about leadership?

2. Where do I need to repent and return to God's mercy?

3. How do I live knowing Messiah is unchanging and ever-present?

4. What spiritual practices help me keep God's Word central?

HA'AZINU

TORAH: DEUTERONOMY 32:1–52
HAFTARA: 2 SAMUEL 22:1–51
NEW TESTAMENT: REVELATION 15:1–8

Moses delivers a poetic song recounting God's faithfulness and Israel's rebellion. The song warns of judgment but also promises God's ultimate vindication of His people. God tells Moses he will die on Mount Nebo for not sanctifying Him at Meribah.

David sings a song of deliverance, praising God as his rock, fortress, and deliverer, echoing Moses' themes of God's faithfulness.

Revelation shows the redeemed singing the Song of Moses and the Song of the Lamb, celebrating God's victory and justice.

CONNECTIONS

- Songs of deliverance unite Moses, David, and the redeemed in Revelation.

- God's faithfulness is constant despite human failure.

- Messiah brings ultimate victory over sin and death.

REFLECTION QUESTIONS

1. How does Moses' song teach me about God's faithfulness?

2. What role does music and praise play in my faith journey?

3. How do I celebrate God's deliverance in my life?

4. What hope do I find in the Song of the Lamb?

VEZOT HABERACHAH

פָּרָשַׁת וְזֹאת הַבְּרָכָה

TORAH: DEUTERONOMY 33:1–34:12
HAFTARA: JOSHUA 1:1–18
NEW TESTAMENT: JUDE 1:24–25

Moses blesses the tribes of Israel before his death. He ascends Mount Nebo, views the Promised Land, and dies there. Joshua takes leadership, and Israel mourns for Moses. The Torah ends with the affirmation of Moses as the greatest prophet in Israel.

Joshua is commissioned to lead Israel into the Promised Land with strength and courage, assured of God's presence.

Jude closes with a doxology, praising God who is able to keep believers from falling and present them blameless with joy in His presence.

CONNECTIONS

- Moses' blessings and farewell echo into Joshua's commission.

- God's presence empowers leadership transitions.

- Messiah secures believers' ultimate blessing and eternal inheritance.

1. What blessings from Moses resonate with me today?

2. How does Joshua's commission encourage me in new seasons?

3. How do I experience God's keeping power in my faith walk?

4. What legacy of faith am I leaving for others?

Closing Reflections and Looking Ahead

As we conclude this year's journey through the Torah, Prophets, and New Testament, we stand in awe of God's faithfulness. From the creation in Bereshit to the blessings of Vezot Haberachah, we have walked with the patriarchs, stood at Sinai, learned the holiness of God, wandered the wilderness, and listened to Moses' final words. Alongside Israel's story, we have seen Messiah Yeshua revealed again and again — the promised Seed, the Lamb, the High Priest, the Living Word.

This cycle has not only taught us information but has shaped us through rhythm. Each week we returned to the Scriptures, joining with God's people worldwide in the same readings. In the process, the Bible has become more than a collection of stories; it has become our life pattern, drawing us deeper into covenant living. We have been reminded that God's Word is alive, forming us into disciples who hear, obey, and reflect His holiness.

As we look forward, the journey does not end here. Jewish tradition teaches that the Torah has no end; when we finish, we begin again. So too in our faith: every cycle uncovers fresh insights, connections, and applications. What was once familiar becomes new, for the Spirit continually illuminates Messiah in the Word. The next year's cycle is not repetition but renewal — another opportunity to encounter God's voice, grow in Yeshua, and deepen our identity as His covenant people.

Therefore, let us carry forward the lessons learned, the reflections written, and the commitments made. May the seeds sown in this year bear fruit in our lives, our families, and our communities. And as we begin the next cycle, may we approach it with anticipation — knowing that God's Word will continue to reveal His covenant love, His Messiah, and His eternal purposes for Israel and the nations.

<u>Closing Reflections</u>

My Key Takeaways from This Year's Cycle:

____

____

____

____

Where I Saw God's Covenant, Messiah, and Israel This Year:

____

____

____

____

Commitments and Action Steps for the Coming Year:

____

____

____

____

My Prayer for the Next Cycle:

____

____

____

____

NEXT YEAR

IN

JERUSALEM